To Holly,
Welcome to the
Neighborhood!
From the Smit
Family

Popcorn Clouds
and
Bubblegum Trees

Devotions for Young Children

Popcorn Clouds
and
Bubblegum Trees

Susan Damon

CRC Publications
Grand Rapids, Michigan

Cover and text illustrations: Scott M. Holladay

The Scripture quotations in this book are from the THE EVERYDAY
BIBLE, NEW CENTURY VERSION. Copyright © 1987, 1988 by Word
Publishing, Dallas, Texas 75039. Used by permission.

Copyright © 1994 CRC Publications, 2850 Kalamazoo Ave. SE, Grand
Rapids, Michigan 49560.

Library of Congress Cataloging-in-Publication Data
Damon, Susan, 1952-
    Popcorn clouds and bubblegum trees: devotions for young children
/ Susan Damon.
      p. cm.
    ISBN 1-56212-076-X
    1. Children—Prayer-books and devotions—English. 2. Christian
life—Juvenile literature. I. Title
    BV4870.D27 1994
    242'.62—dc20   94-40241
                                       CIP
                                       AC

10 9 8 7 6 5 4 3 2

To Mom and Dad,
who by word and example
taught me the ABC's of faith.

A is for Alligator

Alfie and Arnie Alligator were just waddling up from the swamp when they met Rosa the Ranger passing by in her Jeep. "Hi, Arnie!" Rosa called out. "Hi, Alfie!"

"See?" said Arnie, shaking his head in disgust as Rosa disappeared down the trail. "She mixed us up *again!* She still doesn't know that *I'm* Arnie, and *you're* Alfie. Humans can *never* keep us straight!"

Lots of people think alligators look pretty much alike, even alligators that aren't related. But Alfie and Arnie's alligator friends can tell them apart in a second. "Look," they say, "Alfie's and Arnie's eyes are different, their teeth are different, and their skins have different bumps. Even their personalities are different!" Alfie and Arnie can't figure out why humans always confuse them.

But it's not just Alfie and Arnie who are different: every creature in the whole wide world is different from every other creature.

Why do you think that is? Why are creatures so different from each other? It's because God made them that way. And God loves to make his creatures different from each other.

Think of it: all day long, all night long, God watches over our world from heaven. How much fun God must have watching creatures with so many different colors, shapes, and sizes! In the very same jungle he sees the skinny snake and the fat toad, the brightly colored parrot and the little grey mouse.

And think about people. How delighted God must be to see their different skin colors, the different clothes they wear, the different things they say and do. God must smile at their different songs, their different foods, their different homes, their different names. Do you think God ever gets bored?

Watching you, God sees that there is no one else in the world exactly like you. God sees the way you—and only you—wrinkle up your nose or smile at your mom or dad. God knows all the things you like best, and he knows the things you do best. He loves you very much.

And do you know what? God *never* gets you mixed up with anybody else!

PRAISE TIME

Lord, you have examined me. You know all about me. You know when I sit down and when I get up. You know my thoughts before I think them. You know where I go and where I lie down. You know well everything I do.
Psalm 139:1-3

PRAYER TIME

God, thank you for making us all different. Thank you for loving us all the same. Amen.

B is for Bubblegum

Have you ever heard of Betty Bubbles? Why, she can chew the very same piece of bubblegum for days and days and days! At mealtimes, Betty parks her gum behind her ear or on the edge of her plate. At bedtime she places it carefully on her dresser, ready to be chewed first thing the next morning. Because Betty keeps adding fresh pieces, the wad of gum grows bigger and bigger and bigger.

But finally a sad day comes. Betty's precious gum gets all tangled in her hair, or maybe it drops out of her mouth and rolls underneath a dusty couch. Or worse, her teacher notices Betty chewing, and Betty loses both her gum *and* her recess!

From years of chewing, Betty Bubbles has learned something important about bubblegum: at first it tastes great, but after a little while it tastes kind of stale and yucky. That's why Betty has to keep adding new pieces.

Lots of things in life are like bubblegum. New toys, new pets, new games, and new clothes are exciting. But after a while we get tired of them; they get boring. Then we want something else new.

What about God? Is God like bubblegum? Can God get boring?

No! Never! Because every day God has something new to show us, something exciting to teach us.

In God's world, there is so much to learn. Maybe today or tomorrow you'll look closely at a strange bug, a spider's web, a dandelion, or a snowflake. Maybe you'll see a giant oak tree or watch a noisy thunderstorm. Maybe you'll find a new hiding place or a new book or a new friend. God has filled our world with new and interesting things.

Life with God can be fresh and flavorful. Not like old bubblegum! We can go to bed at night happy and content. And we can wake up in the morning eager to see what new things God is waiting to show us.

PRAISE TIME

Lord, you have made me happy by what you have done. I will sing for joy about what your hands have done.
Psalm 92:4

PRAYER TIME

God, life with you is an adventure. We thank you and praise you. Amen.

C is for Color Crayons

"That's not right!" Buffy stared at the picture her older sister, Carrie, was coloring. "You made the grass blue and the sky green. Those aren't the colors they're supposed to be!"

Carrie sighed. "This is *art*," she explained patiently. "When you are the artist, you can make things any way you want."

Carrie picked up a pink crayon. Pink would be for the river, or maybe the sun. She hadn't decided yet.

Carrie is right, isn't she? When you are the artist, you *can* make things any way you want! Just think of the fun colors you could use for people or plants or puppy dogs. Or think of the neat things you could draw.

You could draw a teeny-tiny puppy that would fit into your pocket and go with you everywhere (it would be house-broken). You could make popcorn clouds and bubblegum trees (sugarless, of course). You could draw your mom with six hands, so she could get all her work done. If you have a bald grandpa, you could give him back his hair. Don't you wish you could make things you draw come true?

If you have fun coloring or drawing, just think how much fun God had creating the world! And think how carefully God had to plan everything so the world would come out just right. What if God had put our nostrils on top of our noses? When it rained, we would drown! What if we had no eyebrows? Sweat would run right into our eyes.

If God hadn't created gravity, we would *never* be able to sit in our seats, and then wouldn't our teachers be mad! If earth were a little closer to the sun, we would fry, but if it were a little farther away, we would freeze.

How would Mrs. Giraffe reach her leafy dinner in the trees if God had goofed and given her a short neck? How would Mr. Turtle protect his slow, soft body if God had forgotten his shell?

God made everything just right so his creatures would be safe and comfortable and happy. God is so smart and wise, and such a wonderful artist! He is the best!

PRAISE TIME
Shout to the Lord, all the earth. Serve the Lord with joy. Come before him with singing. Know that the Lord is God. He made us, and we belong to him.
Psalm 100:1-3

PRAYER TIME
God, you are the most wonderful Artist. Thank you for making everything just right. Amen.

D is for Duck Pond

Look, there goes Mama Duck with her eight little ducklings. 'Round and 'round their little pond they go, splashing, diving, floating, paddling, all day long. Watching from shore, Mr. Fox licks his hungry lips. "Hey, Mama Duck!" he calls. "Aren't you tired of swimming around that silly pond all day long? Come up on shore and have some fun!"

Mama Duck scoops up a juicy green water plant with her bill and laughs. "No thanks," she says. "I've got my family and food and everything I need right here. I am one happy duck!"

Still smiling, Mama Duck tosses the plant to little Dabble Duckling, who nips off a bit and passes it on. Each duckling waits patiently for its turn to eat. When they're done eating, they all say, "Thank you, Mama. That was good!"

"I've saved some for Papa," says Diddle, the last duckling.

"That's nice," says Mama Duck. "Papa will be hungry after he flies back from visiting Aunt Flo."

"Drat!" says Mr. Fox, rubbing his empty belly. "I might as well go home and have a piece of toast."

The moment Mr. Fox steps inside his den, Brother Fox says, "What took you so long? We're starving!"

"Where's the duck?" snaps Mrs. Fox. "You promised!"

"I know, dear," says Mr. Fox, "but ducks are not easy to catch."

"It's toast again," complains Brother Fox. "We had toast last night."

"Yeah, and you ate all the honey," complains Sister Fox.

"I did not!" snarls Brother Fox.

"You did so!" whines Sister Fox.

"Stop it this instant!" barks Mrs. Fox.

Quietly, Mr. Fox sneaks out the back door to order a pizza. Then he eats the whole pizza himself.

Well, which home would *you* rather live in—Mama Duck's pond or Mr. Fox's den?

God hates things like fighting, teasing, and complaining, because he knows how unhappy they make us. Can you think of things God *likes* to see in our homes—things that make God (and us!) happy?

PRAISE TIME

It is good and pleasant when God's people
live together in peace!
Psalm 133:1

PRAYER TIME

God, thank you for our home. Help us to make
our home a safe and happy place. Amen.

E is for Eraser

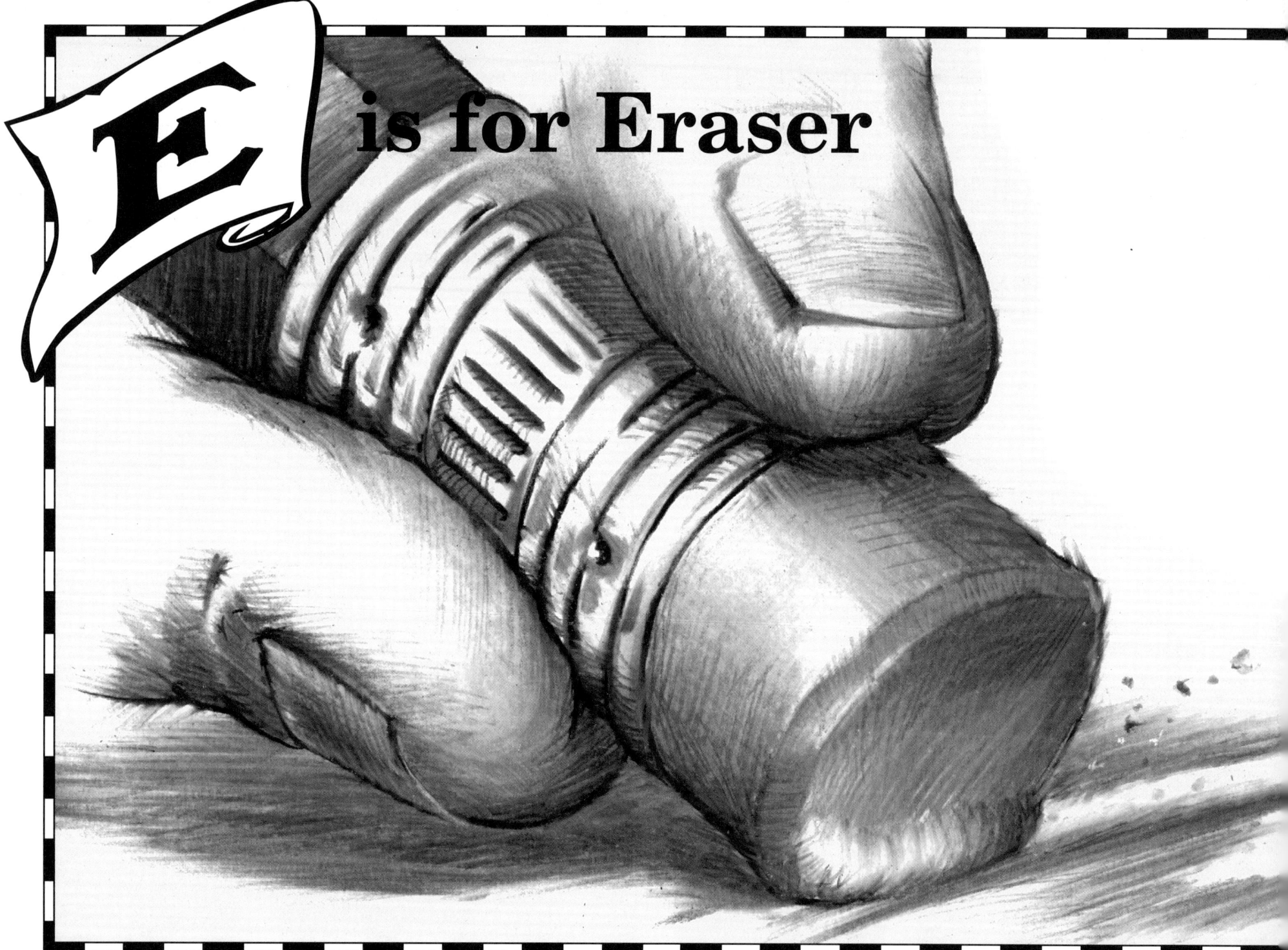

Eddie sits at his desk, erasing. Erasing and scowling, because Eddie is mad! His paper is full of red checks where he added wrong. Three plus four is not eight. Eleven plus three is not fifteen. Now he has to erase all the wrong answers and fix them up—during recess! Rub, rub, rub goes Eddie. Rub, rub, RRRRIP! Now Eddie is really mad. He'll have to do the whole page over. That will take two recesses at least!

Eddie stares at the little pink piece of rubber in his hand. It's almost used up from all the rubbing it has to do, and there are eraser crumbs all over his desk. He brushes them onto the floor.

I hate this, thinks Eddie. *It wouldn't be so bad if I could add and subtract as well as my older sister. And it wouldn't be so bad if I didn't always have to fix my mistakes and miss recess! I wish I had a magic eraser, thinks Eddie. I wish I had a magic eraser that would rub off all the mistakes with one swipe, and not even wrinkle the paper.*

A magic eraser—now there's an idea. Just think what you could do with a magic eraser! You could get rid of all kinds of mistakes, mistakes like calling your teacher "Mom" in front of the whole class. You could get rid of accidents too, accidents like knocking over the applesauce-jar display at the supermarket.

What if you could even erase sins, the wrong things you do that make you feel so bad? Eddie could think of lots of sins he'd like to get rid of. Like the time he'd punched his sister so hard in church that she'd cried—out loud—and everyone looked at him, even the minister. Or when he'd called his mom a really bad word he'd heard at a hockey game. Oh, a magic eraser that could get rid of things like that would be wonderful!

What about you? Do you ever feel like Eddie? Have you done things you feel bad about, things you wish you could erase forever? Do you ever wish you had a magic eraser? Actually, in a way you do.

Whenever you do something bad, no matter how bad, you can go to God. You can say, "God, I know I did something wrong, and I'm really sorry. Will you forgive me?" Then God will look at you and he'll look at Jesus. And he'll say to Jesus, "Son, did you die for that sin too?" Then Jesus will look at you and say to God, "Yes, Father, I died for that sin too. This is my child!" And then it's as if God takes out his eraser and rubs you so clean that you can't even see a mark where the sin was. It's all gone!

God knows that all of us sin over and over again. But God is always ready to erase our sins if we tell him we're sorry. And God's eraser never gets used up!

PRAISE TIME

God, be merciful to me because you are loving. Because you are always ready to be merciful, wipe out all my wrongs.
Psalm 51:1

PRAYER TIME

God, we do wrong things every day. Please forgive us and make us clean again. Amen.

F is for Firefly

On a warm summer evening, when it's dark, Frannie Firefly flits across the dark backyard at Grandma's house. Frannie's tiny light flashes on and off, on and off, like a mini-flashlight. Staring into the darkness, Kim and her brother Michael don't really see Frannie because it is too dark. They see only her little light, and they never know where they will see it next.

"There it is, over by the bushes!" Kim shouts. "No, now it's over by the tree!"

"Look!" shouts Michael. "I just saw another firefly by the garage."

Kim and Michael are up late because they can't get to sleep. Grandma comes outside to check on them. "Don't be so loud," she scolds. "You'll wake up the whole neighborhood!"

"Grandma, you should see the fireflies!" exclaims Kim. "I wish I could put them in a jar and take them to bed with me. If I had a whole bunch, I wouldn't need a nightlight, and I wouldn't be so scared of the dark."

"Is that why you can't get to sleep?" asks Grandma. "Is it because you're scared?"

"Uh-huh," says Kim.

"I'm not scared," says Michael.

"Then why do you always go to sleep with your light on?" Kim asks Michael.

Grandma gives Kim and Michael a hug. "Sometimes I'm afraid of the dark too," she says. "But you know, when God made darkness, he meant it to be our friend. God gave the daytime the big bright sun, so we could see to work and play and eat and do all the things we need to do. But he made the night dark, so the earth would slow down and be quiet and rest."

"But the moon and stars shine at night," Kim says.

"That's true," says Grandma. "I think God gave us those beautiful soft lights at night to remind us that he is always with us, even in the darkness. Sometimes at night I lie in my bed, all snug and warm, and I look up at the stars through my window, and I talk to God. Then God seems very close, and the darkness feels safe and cozy."

"I talk to God at night too," Kim says. "But I still like my nightlight on."

"I'm sure God understands," Grandma says, smiling.

"I'm sure he does too," giggles Franny Firefly, passing by. "Who do you think gave me *my* nightlight?"

PRAISE TIME

The Lord shows his true love every day. At night I have a song, and I pray to my living God.
Psalm 42:8

PRAYER TIME

God, thank you for night when we can rest.
Stay close to us while we sleep.
Help us to not be afraid. Amen.

G is for Garbage

Greg was awakened by the roar of a motor. A huge garbage truck was backing up to his open bedroom window. Closer and closer came the mountain of garbage—broken bottles, chicken bones, and slimy banana peels. The smell was sickening—it made Greg want to throw up.

When the truck was right up against the window it stopped. A big man in overalls jumped out. "Okay!" he shouted to someone in the truck. "Let 'er go!"

"Hey!" screeched Greg. "Not in my room!"

The big man in overalls looked up in surprise. "Oh, sorry, kid," he said. "Someone said your room was a dump."

Elizabeth! thought Greg angrily. *I'll bet it was her!* Greg's sister Elizabeth always kept her room perfectly clean and tidy. She never got sick of telling everyone that Greg's room was a dump.

"I don't care what anyone says," shouted Greg. "My room is not a dump!"

The man stuck his head in through the window. The floor of Greg's room was littered with dirty socks and underwear. On the bed were cookie crumbs and a half-eaten bag of chips. "Well, okay—if you say so," the man said. But then where *is* the dump?"

"Well," said Greg, "take a left at the next corner and keep going till you hit the smell. You can't miss it!"

"Thanks, kid," said the man. He climbed back into the truck, and off it roared.

"Phew!" said Greg, slamming his window shut and climbing back into bed. "That was close!"

Greg couldn't get back to sleep. He lay wide awake, thinking about his awful experience and plotting revenge on his sister. Suddenly his thoughts were interrupted by a noise like thunder that came from the direction of the dump. It was a voice from heaven. The voice boomed, "Hey! Don't dump that junk in my room!" It was God's voice!

Greg woke up on the floor. Fortunately, he had fallen onto a soft pile of dirty socks and underwear. "Wow, what a dream!" he said. "Thank goodness it wasn't real!"

At breakfast Greg told his family about his dream. "I never thought about it like that before," he said. "Polluting the air and the water and dumping bad chemicals and junk around on the earth is like dumping garbage in God's room. God made the earth, so it's all his. I'll bet it makes him pretty mad when we do that!"

"I'll bet it does," agreed Dad.

"I'm not going to litter or waste stuff anymore!" said Greg. "At least I'll try not to. At school we're learning lots of ways to help take care of the earth. There are all kinds of things I can do."

"You could start by cleaning your room," said Elizabeth.

"I already did," said Greg. "Go and check it out!"

PRAISE TIME
The earth and everything in it
belong to the Lord.
Psalm 24:1

PRAYER TIME
God, we are sorry about messing up your world. Teach us to care about your world as much as you do. Amen.

H

is for Helmet

As you climb onto the brand-new Harley-Davidson motorcycle, you are excited—really excited. You know what your mom would say: "No child of mine is ever going to ride one of those!" But you don't care. You are staying for a whole week with your Uncle Stanley, and Uncle Stanley does not treat you like a baby. You roar off down the street. Unfortunately, you have forgotten that Uncle Stanley's street has speed bumps. You hit a bump and go sailing head over heels through the air. Before you land you think, *Mom was right. Good thing I'm wearing my helmet!*

After you get out of the hospital, you decide to try something a little less dangerous. So you enter the Great Downhill Mountain Bike Race. You are the last one to race, and you must beat the time of last year's winner, Lightning Leroy. As you zip down the mountainside, you can hear the cheers of the crowd below. You know that, wonder of wonders, you are winning. Suddenly, from out of nowhere, a mountain goat leaps across your path. You swerve and lose control! As you roll head over heels down the mountain, you think, *Good thing I'm wearing my helmet!*

After you get out of the hospital, you want to try something without wheels. You are invited to join your favorite major-league baseball team. It's the last inning of your first game. Your team is behind by one run, there are two outs, and you are up to bat. The pitcher for the other team is Wild Willy, the worst pitcher in the league. His first pitch is a fastball, whizzing straight toward your head. There's no time to duck. As you lie sprawled in the dirt, you think, *Good thing I'm wearing my helmet!* When you get out of the hospital this time, you will try something safe, like knitting.

Wearing a helmet is an important way to protect our brains. And what in the world would we do without them? Without our brains, we wouldn't be able to see or talk or run or think or *anything.* Our hearts would stop beating and our lungs would stop breathing. We wouldn't be alive!

God gave us two legs, two hands, two eyes, two ears, two mouths—well, maybe not two mouths!—but only one brain. If any part of our brain gets hurt, some other part of us won't work right. Our brains are very precious.

Sometimes it seems like a nuisance and a bother to wear a helmet when we ride our bikes or play sports. But wearing a helmet is a good way to protect the precious gift God hid inside our heads. And it is a good way to say, "Thank you, God. Thank you for my brain!"

PRAISE TIME
I praise you because you made me
in an amazing and wonderful way.
Psalm 139:14

PRAYER TIME
God, thank you for our wonderful
brains. Thank you for helmets to
protect our brains. Amen.

I

is for Icicle

Ian, Boy Explorer, sits before a blazing fire in a little log cabin, sipping a cup of hot chocolate. His sled dogs are snoozing at his feet. He is on his way to the Arctic. But right now he is snowed in—outside a blizzard is raging, and all Ian can do is wait for it to end. When the storm is over, he will dig himself out and be on his way.

Looking out the window, all Ian can see are huge icicles hanging off the roof. He remembers watching a TV program that showed how icicles grow, drop by tiny drop, as little bits of melted snow run down the icicle and freeze again at the tip. He wonders how long it took for the icicles outside his window to get this big. Probably a long time.

Ian starts to think about other things that take a long time. He remembers his little sister, Belinda, learning to walk. First she stood up, hanging onto the side of her crib. Then she stood alone, and everyone clapped and said how smart she was. Then she walked around holding onto Ian's fingers, and then—finally—she took a couple of steps on her own. Belinda fell down a lot at first, so it was a good thing she wore diapers.

Ian also remembers learning to read. That took a long time too. It seemed like everyone in his class learned faster than he did. When he looked at a book, the letters seemed to jump around and mix themselves up. Sometimes he would get so frustrated that he would cry. Then his mom would say, "Don't give up! You're getting better and better, I can tell. You're absolutely the best Boy Explorer I know." And that would make Ian feel a little better.

Then Ian remembers a children's sermon he heard last week in church. The minister talked about how long it takes to learn to be a Christian. He said it takes your whole life!

Sometimes Ian feels like a good Christian—once he let his little sister, Belinda, have his balloon because she sat on hers and popped it. Other times he feels like a rotten Christian, like the time he lied to his mom about having his homework done, or the time he punched James in the eye and had to go to the principal, or the time he broke his grandma's favorite candy dish and didn't tell her. When he does bad things, Ian feels he will never learn to be a good Christian.

But don't give up, the minister had said, because God never, ever gives up on us. God never stops loving us, even when we've done something completely rotten. He never gets tired of forgiving us when we are sorry. And he is always ready to help us try again.

Ian really wants to be a good Christian, even if it takes a whole lot longer than it takes to make a million icicles. He decides he will tell his grandma about the candy dish—as soon as he gets back from the Arctic!

PRAISE TIME
The Lord gives strength to those who are tired. He gives more power to those who are weak.
Isaiah 40:29

PRAYER TIME
God, we do want to follow you. Thank you for being so patient with us while we learn.
Amen.

J is for Jack and Jill

McKenzie Kite was the best-looking kite in the neighborhood, and he knew it. He was a magnificent green dragon with flaming red eyes and fire spewing from his mouth. Whenever McKenzie was flying, everyone looked up and exclaimed, "Ooohh! Look at that kite!"

But McKenzie Kite was not happy, not at all! He hated the string that kept him tied to earth. He longed to be free. He longed to soar above the clouds, maybe even past the sun. Oh, the places McKenzie would go, if only he were free!

One blustery day, McKenzie's wish came true. A sudden gust of wind caught him and snapped his string. *Wheeee!* thought McKenzie. *Free at last!*

But what happened next was not what McKenzie had expected. Instead of going where he wanted, poor McKenzie found himself being tossed and blown every which way. He was not free at all; he was a prisoner of the wind!

Looking down, McKenzie saw with alarm that the ground was getting closer and closer. Poor McKenzie! Down, down he went, until—CRASH! Now McKenzie was the worst-looking kite in the neighborhood—and he knew it.

Sometimes rules feel like kite strings. They hold us back and keep us from doing what we want to do. We wish there were no rules; we wish we could be free.

It's true that not all rules are good. People sometimes make bad rules, because people are not perfect. But God's rules, God's laws, are always good, just as God is good.

Think about just one of God's rules, "You shall not steal." Wouldn't it be nice to go into stores and take whatever we want, like candy bars and computer games? But what if everyone did that? It wouldn't be long before there would be nothing left for people to buy. And what was left would be locked up and guarded by very large and very mean dogs. Think of what a bad place our world would be if everyone broke God's rule against stealing.

God's rules make our world a better place to live. They keep us from hurting ourselves and other people. And they teach us to do what's right. Jesus said, "Treat other people the way you would like them to treat you." Think what a wonderful place our world would be if everyone followed those rules!

God has given us rules that we need to be safe and happy. And he has written those rules in the Bible, so we won't forget them. What a good and wise ruler God is! He must love us very much!

PRAISE TIME

The Lord's rules can be trusted. They make plain people wise.
Psalm 19:7

PRAYER TIME

God, thank you for your rules. We love you and want to obey you. Please help us. Amen.

L is for Lizard

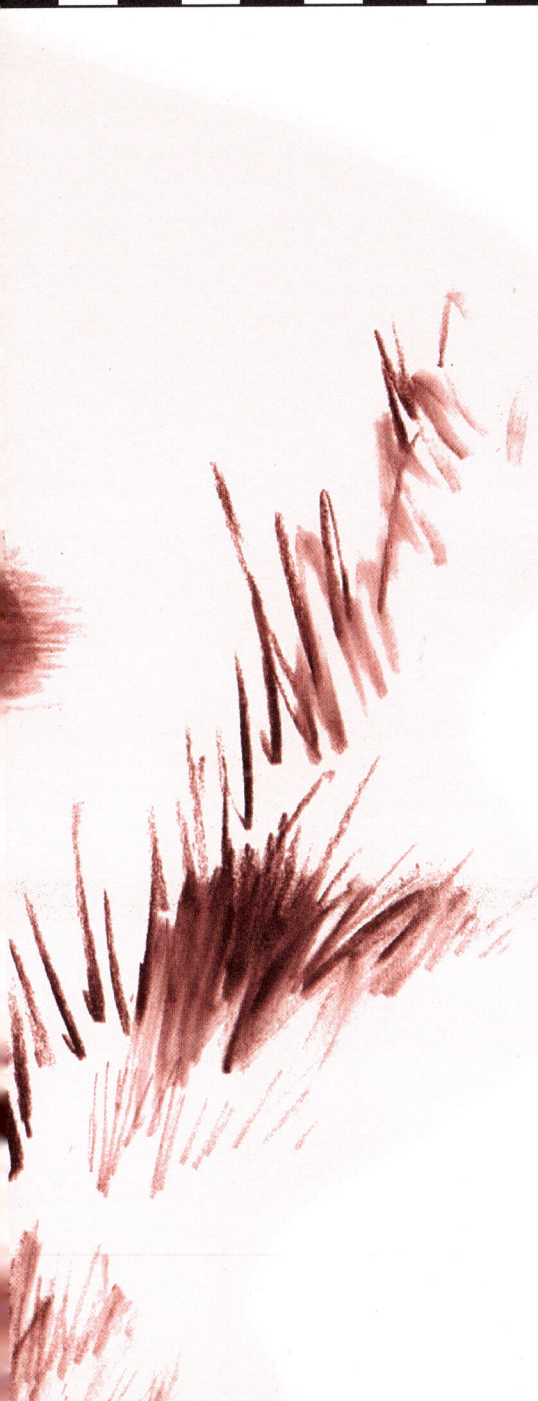

Lisa was out walking with her mother. Suddenly two small creatures skittered across their path.

"EEEEEK!" shrieked Lisa.

"Don't be scared," said Lisa's mother. "They're only lizards."

"But they're so ugly," said Lisa. "Look at their bulgy little eyes and bumpy skin."

"They're not ugly," said Lisa's mother. "They're just a different kind from us. I'm sure other lizards think they look very nice."

Lizzie Lizard was out walking with *her* mother. Suddenly two enormous creatures crossed their path.

"EEEEEK!" shrieked Lizzie.

"Don't be scared," said Lizzie's mother. "They're only humans."

"But they're so ugly," said Lizzie. "Their skin is so smooth, and they have strings growing out of their heads."

"Those aren't strings; they're hair," said Lizzie's mother, "and humans aren't ugly. They're just a different kind from us. I'm sure that to other humans they look quite lovely."

The Bible tells us that God made lizards and God made people—and God made everything else in our world that walks or talks or flies or swims. This is *God*'s world.

It doesn't make any difference to God if we are tall or short, male or female, brown, black, or white. If we love Jesus, then we belong to God, and God sees us all as his beautiful children.

Is there something about yourself that you don't like, that you wish you could change? Maybe you wish you were taller or shorter or skinnier or quicker, or that you had bigger muscles. Maybe you don't like your hair or your teeth or your ears. Maybe you can't speak clearly, or your legs don't work well and you have to use a wheelchair or wear braces. Maybe you have scars from an accident, or maybe it takes you longer to learn things. Maybe people who don't understand stare at you or make fun of you.

God would never do that, not ever! No matter what anyone else says about you, and no matter what you say about yourself, God looks at you and says, "You are beautiful! I love you. You belong to me."

PRAISE TIME
Know that the Lord is God.
He made us, and we belong
to him.
Psalm 100:3

PRAYER TIME
God, thank you for loving us
just the way we are. Help us
to be like you in loving
others. Amen.

M is for Mud

Most grownups don't like mud very much. Poor grown ups! They have to spend so much time getting rid of mud—from cars and clothes and floors—that they don't have time for the fun things you can do with mud: You can draw in it with a stick, you can make mud pies, you can squish it between your bare toes. You can even pick it up and let it ooze through your fingers. It's a good thing God made kids, or there'd be nobody to like mud!

Palestine—the land where Jesus grew up—has its share of mud too. Probably Jesus played in the mud sometimes, like the other kids in the neighborhood. And when Jesus grew up, he spent three years tramping up and down the dirt roads of the countryside. The dust and dirt on those roads turned to soupy mud whenever it rained. So Jesus and his disciples knew what mud felt like on their sandals and feet.

One day, as Jesus was walking along, he saw a man who had been blind all of his life. In those days, people who were blind weren't allowed to work like everyone else. Instead, they had to sit by a road or outside a building all day long, begging for money from people who passed by. How boring!

Perhaps the blind man expected to receive some money from Jesus. But instead of money, Jesus gave him mud! That's right—mud.

Jesus spit on the ground. Then he bent down and made some mud with the saliva. He took the mud and put it on the blind man's eyes. Can't you just hear the grownups: "Oooooooh, yuk! Mud!" It's a good thing the blind man's mom and dad weren't there. They might have said, "Just look at you! You've got mud all over your face!"

But the man who was blind didn't care. He wanted so badly to see, and he believed that Jesus could help him. After Jesus put the mud on the blind man's eyes, he said to him, "Go and wash in the Pool of Siloam." The blind man did exactly what Jesus told him to do. He went and washed—and he could see! Imagine that!

Was the mud magic? Was it a special mud that could do miracles? No, the mud was just mud. But Jesus was a very special person. He was God, and God can do anything, even with mud!

PRAISE TIME

No God is as great as our God. You are the God who did miracles. You showed people your power.
Psalm 77:13-14

PRAYER TIME

God, you show your power in everything, even in mud. We praise you. Amen.

N is for Nasty

One morning Ned woke up feeling *nasty*. As he stomped downstairs for breakfast, he kicked over the pile of clean laundry his mom had left on the bottom stair. Stomping through the living room, he knocked over the block castle his little brother had worked over an hour to build. He stomped into the kitchen and flopped down at the table. His dad, stirring a pot on the stove, looked up in surprise and said, "Well! Good morning, Ned."

"Humph!" said Ned. "I hate oatmeal."

"It tastes good with a little butter and sugar," said Dad.

Ned grabbed the sugar bowl. He turned it upside down and dumped the whole bowl of sugar on his cereal. "That's enough!" said Dad. "Go to your room!"

Ned stomped back upstairs to his room, slammed the door behind him, and threw himself onto his bed.

Suddenly he heard a small voice inside him. "Ned!" said the voice. "Feeling a little nasty?"

Oh, no! It was God! God was the last person Ned wanted to talk to right now.

"So," said God, "what are we going to do about your being nasty?"

"Well," said Ned hopefully, "you could take my nasties away."

God chuckled. "I could," he said, "but that would be sort of a waste of all the ways I've given you to help yourself."

"Like what?" asked Ned in surprise.

"Think about it," said God.

Ned thought. "You mean like I could take a nap?" he asked.

"A good idea for later on," answered God. "What about right now?"

Ned thought again. "You mean like eat a good breakfast and be nice to my dad?"

"Another good idea," said God.

"But Dad won't let me eat breakfast," said Ned. "You saw what I did."

"He might change his mind," said God.

"Well," said Ned slowly, "maybe if I picked up the stuff I knocked over, and apologized."

"Try it!" said God. "Oh, and Ned, there's one more thing."

"I know, God. I should apologize to you too. I really am sorry. Will you forgive me?"

"You're forgiven," said God. "Now let's see about getting you some breakfast!"

"You mean you'll go with me?" asked Ned.

"I'm always with you, Ned," God said quietly. "Even when you're nasty!"

O is for Orange

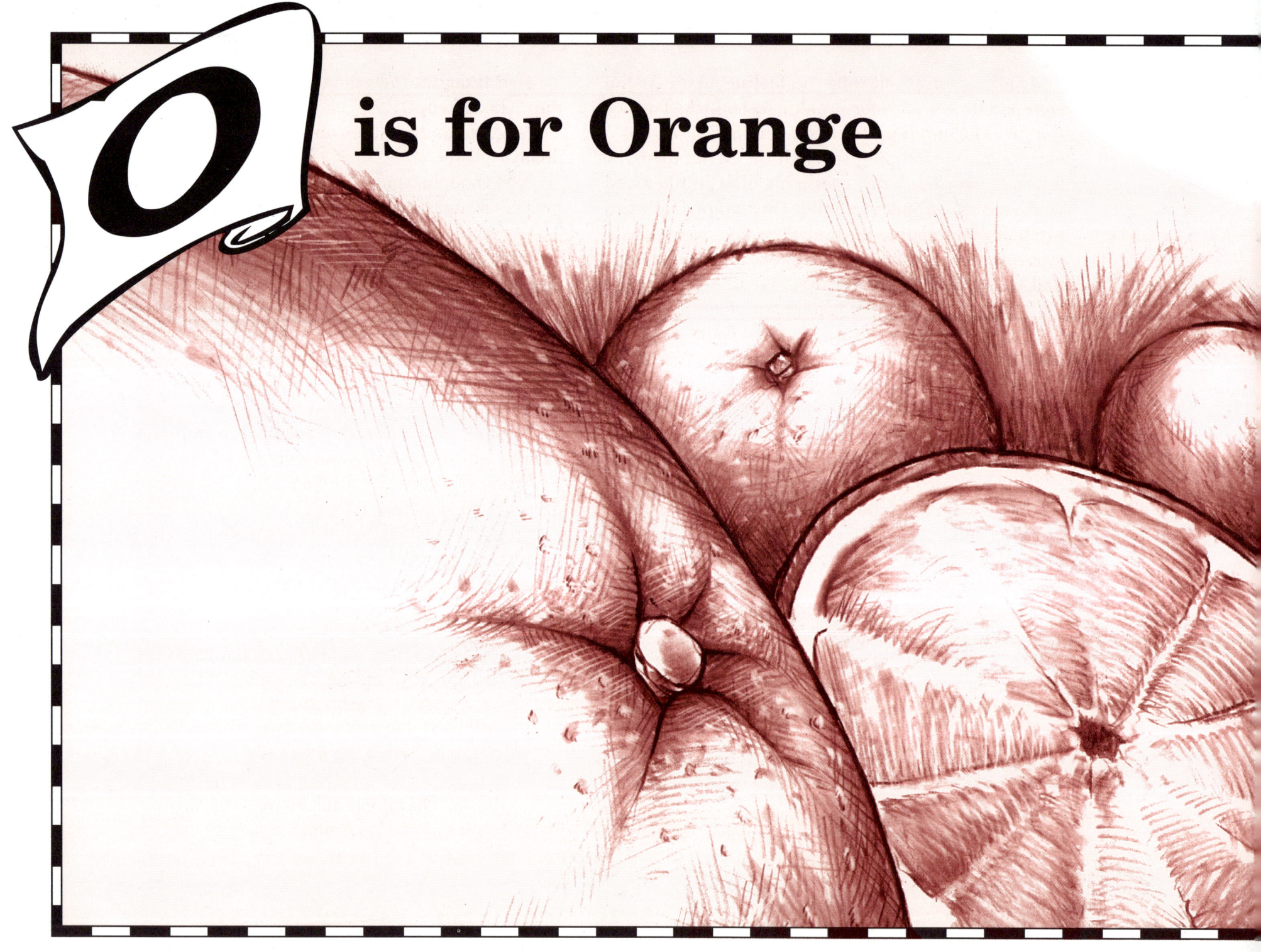

It was Olive and Orville Orangutan's very first breakfast in the Garden of Eden. What fun they were having, swinging through the garden, trying the different fruits God had made! Already they'd tasted apples, peaches, cherries, and pears. And they loved them all.

"Hey, here's a different fruit," said Orville, plucking something with bumpy orange skin from a branch overhead. He took a big bite . . . and quickly spit it out. "EEEEWWW!" he exclaimed, making a horrible face. "It's so bitter!" Orville handed the fruit to Olive. "Here, try it," he said.

"No, thank you," answered Olive, looking at Orville's face. "I believe you." Olive looked puzzled. "I wonder why God made *that* fruit," she said. "Why would God make something that tastes so bad?"

Just then, along came an elephant with a monkey riding high on her back. "Look," exclaimed the elephant. "More oranges!"

"Oh, stop! Please get me one!" squealed the monkey. With her trunk, the elephant plucked a large, beautiful orange from the tree and dropped it to the ground. Up went her huge foot, then down, and SMUSH went the orange. With a shriek of delight, the monkey leaped off the elephant's back, swooped up the orange, and began gobbling the insides.

Orville looked at Olive. Olive looked at Orville. "Hmmmm," said Orville, scratching his head thoughtfully, "maybe if we took off the skin. . . ."

The elephant plucked another orange from the tree. "May I peel it for you, Madam?" she asked Olive with a smile.

"No thank you," said Olive politely. "I think I'd like mine a little less smushed!"

Just think how boring it would be if we had to eat the same food at every meal every day for our whole lives. God could have done that, you know. He could have made just one kind of food for everybody to eat all the time.

But God isn't like that. He doesn't just want his creatures to stay alive. He wants us to enjoy being alive. So he filled the earth with food of every kind—vegetables, meats, fish, grains, fruits, nuts, and berries. God made sweet foods, sour foods, crunchy foods, and mushy foods.

Like Orville and Olive Orangutan, we can have fun trying the different foods God has given us. God knows we won't like some foods, even if we take off the peels. After all, it's God who made us all different. But every time we discover a new food we like, we can thank our wonderful God.

PRAISE TIME

God wants everyone to eat and drink and be happy in his work. These are gifts from God.
Ecclesiastes 3:13

PRAYER TIME

God, thank you that eating can be so much fun. Amen.

P is for Pancake

"Where are you going, Aristotle?" asked Aristotle's father.

"Far, far away," answered Aristotle. "I'm going exploring."

"Well, be careful," said Aristotle's father. "Don't fall off the earth!"

Fall off the earth? Yikes! Aristotle hadn't thought about that. In those days, many years ago, almost everyone thought the earth was flat, like a pancake. They were sure that if you traveled too far in one direction you would fall right off the edge of the earth. And no one knew what might happen to you then!

Maybe I won't go exploring after all, thought Aristotle. *Maybe I'll just go down to the sea.*

As Aristotle sat on the seashore, watching the ships come and go, he thought about what might happen if you fell off the earth. Do great monsters hide under the earth, waiting to gobble you up? Would you just keep falling and falling forever?

Aristotle saw a ship far out at sea, almost to the horizon, where sky and water meet. Suddenly Aristotle had a scary thought. What if the horizon really were the edge of the world? What if that ship were about to fall off? All the sailors would be lost!

Leaping to his feet, Aristotle began waving his arms and shouting frantically. "Watch out, watch out!" he shouted, but, of course, no one in the ship could hear him. Aristotle could hardly bear to watch. Any moment now, the ship might drop right out of sight.

As Aristotle watched, the ship *did* disappear, but not suddenly, as Aristotle had expected. Instead, it disappeared very slowly, first the bottom and then the sails, as though it were gliding down a gently sloping hill. *That's strange,* thought Aristotle. Could everyone, even his father, be wrong? Maybe the earth was not flat after all!

Today we laugh to think that people used to believe the earth was flat as a pancake. After all, we have pictures of the earth, taken from space, and we know very well that the earth is round, like a big, beautiful ball. But a hundred years from now, people will laugh at some of the things *we* think. And two hundred years from now, people will laugh at the people who laughed at us.

That's because human beings will never, ever know everything. It's a good thing too. Life would be pretty boring if there were nothing new to discover. Besides, if we humans knew everything, we might think we didn't need God. We might think we were smart enough to take care of ourselves. And then we would really be in big trouble!

"P" is for pancake, which we know is *not* the shape of the earth. "P" is also for praise. Praise to God, the only one who knows everything, because he made it all!

PRAISE TIME

Trust the Lord with all your heart. Don't depend on your own understanding.
Proverbs 3:5

PRAYER TIME

God, you know everything, and we know so little. We praise you. Amen.

Q is for Quiet

Queenie heard them even before they got inside the house. She heard them rattling the front door lock with their burglar tools, and she tore upstairs to warn her master.

"Bark bark—bark bark bark bark!" said Queenie.

Queenie's master, Gordon, was snuggled comfortably in bed, reading an exciting murder mystery. "Quiet, Queenie!" said Gordon.

Queenie tore back downstairs. The burglars were already in the house, heading straight for the famous million-dollar painting hanging in the living room. Queenie tore back upstairs. "Bark bark bark—bark bark bark bark!" said Queenie.

"Quiet, Queenie!" said Gordon. "I'm trying to read!"

Queenie tore back downstairs. The burglars were just coming out of the bathroom with Gordon's rubber ducky, the one he'd had since he was a little boy. It was still his favorite bath toy. Back upstairs raced Queenie. "BARK BARK BARK BARK BARK—BARK BARK BARK BARK!" she said.

"BE QUIET, Queenie," said Gordon. "I told you I'm trying to read!"

Back downstairs raced Queenie. Now the burglars were in the kitchen, removing a large ham from the fridge. That was too much for Queenie—that ham bone was hers!

Up the stairs tore Queenie, barking furiously all the way. "BARK BARK BARK BARK BARK BARK BARK!" said Queenie. She raced into Gordon's room, yanked the covers off his bed, and nipped him on a big, hairy toe.

"OUCH! QUIT IT, QUEENIE!" shouted Gordon. But Queenie just stood there and barked for all she was worth. "Oh, all right," said Gordon with a sigh. "I suppose you're hungry. Let's go get a snack."

Queenie tore down the stairs ahead of her master, but it was too late: the burglars were just disappearing out the front door. Queenie barked furiously at the closed door, then sank to the floor in a sad little heap.

From the kitchen came Gordon's loud wail: "My ham! It's been stolen!" Then from the living room came a louder wail: "My famous million-dollar painting! It's been stolen!" And finally, from the bathroom, came the loudest wail of all: "MY RUBBER DUCKY! IT'S BEEN STOLEN! QUEENIE, WHY DIDN'T YOU WARN ME?" Queenie just shook her head. People could be so dumb!

Sometimes we are like Queenie's master. When we do something wrong, God tries to warn us, the way little Queenie tried to warn Gordon. "Watch out!" God says. "What you are doing is wrong! Stop, before you get hurt, and other people do too!"

Will we listen to God and stop the wrong thing we are doing? Or will we tell God to be quiet and hope he'll go away?

God will not go away. We can shut our ears, but like Queenie, God will keep on warning us. God loves us too much to be quiet!

PRAISE TIME

[The Lord] is our God. And we are the people he takes care of. . . . Today, listen to what he says.
Psalm 95:7

PRAYER TIME

God, thank you for warning us when we do wrong. Please help us to listen. Amen.

R is for Rice*

Mother Teresa loved Jesus more than anything in the world. She could not stand to see poor people dying on the streets of India with no one to love them or care for them. So she started a home for them to stay in. You might think a home for dying people would be a sad and gloomy place, but this home was not. In this home, the love of Jesus brightened and warmed every corner.

For twenty-five years the Home for the Dying took care of people who had nowhere else to go. It was time to celebrate!

So Mother Teresa went to some rich women and said, "We are having a party. Please prepare food for our people. And please, come serve it to them yourselves."

The rich women drove to the home for the dying in big cars. They brought lots of good food—rice, chicken curry, potatoes, curds, bananas, and oranges.

Mother Teresa smiled as she watched the rich women in their fancy dresses kneel beside the poor people in ragged clothing, offering them food. She knew Jesus was smiling too.

One of Mother Teresa's helpers filled a plate with rice and a little chicken and brought it to a man lying flat on a couch. The man was too weak to sit up or even to move his arms.

"Will you eat?" asked Mother Teresa's helper.

"Yes," answered the man on the couch.

"What is your name?"

"Dhinenraj."

"How old are you?"

"I don't know."

"How long have you been here?"

"Four days."

"Where did you come from?"

"I was on the street."

"What is your sickness?"

"My stomach is completely flat, quite empty."

The man's sickness was hunger. Who knew how long he had gone without food before Mother Teresa's helpers had found him?

The hungry man opened his mouth wide, and the helper fed him. With great pleasure the man ate every last bit of food on his plate.

"You have not had a meal like this since you were a boy, or maybe since your wedding feast," said Mother Teresa's helper, with a smile. The man on the couch smiled back.

It was just a simple meal, rice and a little chicken. But to the hungry man it was a taste of heaven. For in heaven, poor people will never again be hungry, and rich and poor people together will celebrate the love of Jesus.

PRAISE TIME

A generous person will be blessed because he shares his food with the poor.
Proverbs 22:9

PRAYER TIME

God, you have given us so much. Thank you for the joy of sharing with others who have less. Amen.

*Based on a story in Mother Teresa of Calcutta: A Biography, by Edward Le Joly, Harper & Row, San Francisco, 1977, 1983

S is for Sugar

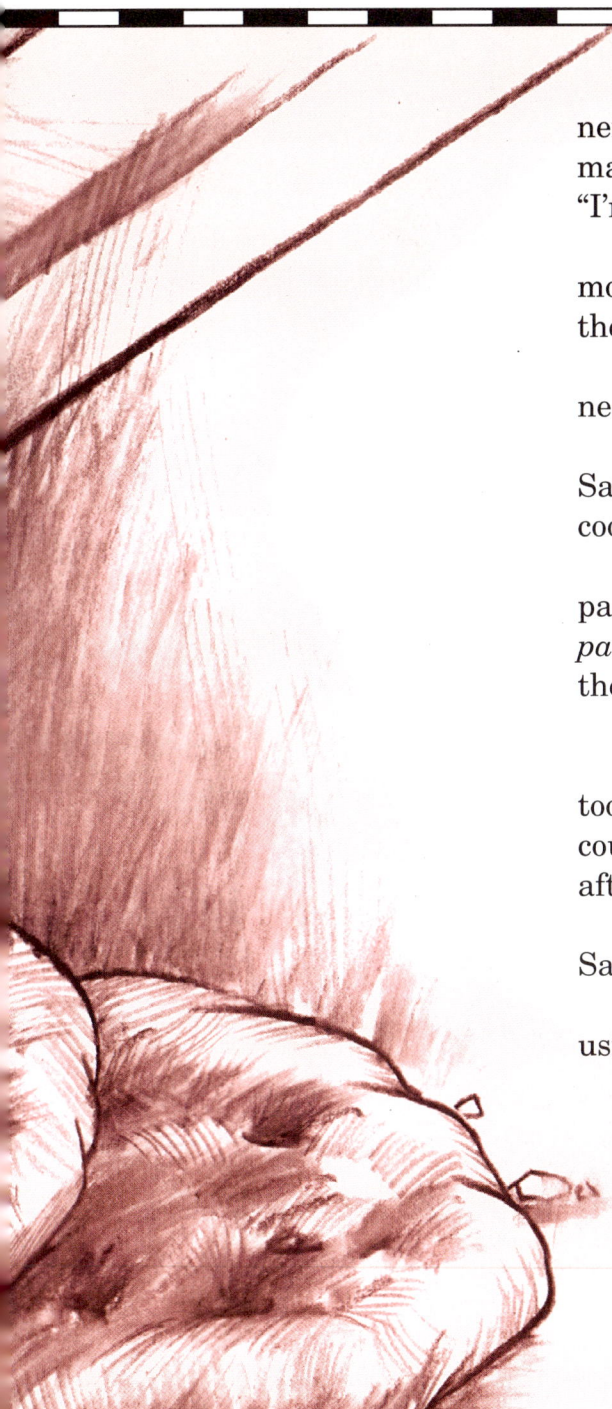

"You must be new in the neighborhood," said the pleasant-faced man behind the counter at Sam's Grocery. "I'm Sam."

"I'm Sarah," said Sarah. "We just moved into the apartment building across the street two days ago."

"Welcome," said Sam. "What do you need?"

"I need a package of sugar," said Sarah. "My mom and I are making cookies, and we ran out."

"Ah!" exclaimed Sam. "You don't need a package of sugar. You need the sugar *package!* A sugar *package* is sugar *plus* all the things you'll need with it."

"Like what?" asked Sarah.

"Like this," said Sam. He pulled a toothbrush out from underneath the counter. "You'll need to brush your teeth after you've eaten those sugary cookies!"

"I could use a new toothbrush," said Sarah. "My old one is getting worn out."

"Good!" said Sam. "That means you're using it!"

Sam pulled out a little booklet and held it up. Sarah read the title: *101 Facts About Sugar.* "This will tell you all the good and bad things about different kinds of sugar," said Sam.

"Is that it?" asked Sarah. "Is that the whole sugar package?"

"Nope," said Sam, suddenly looking serious. "There's one more thing. It's very important." From a cupboard he pulled a big book with a shiny black cover. "This is a Bible. It reminds us that whenever God gives us something, he wants us to use it carefully and to share it with others. I've marked verses for you to read."

"Thank you," said Sarah. "We don't have a Bible. But hey, if I'm supposed to share, shall I share a few cookies with you after they're baked?"

"That would be great!" said Sam, putting the toothbrush, the booklet, the Bible, and a package of sugar into a bag for Sarah to take home. "And when you come back, I'll show you the spinach package!"

PRAISE TIME
What can I give the Lord for all the good things he has given to me?
Psalm 116:12

PRAYER TIME
God, thank you for all your gifts. Amen.

T is for Toenails

"Please, Teacher, may I be first for show-and-tell?" pleaded Porcupine.

"Sure you may," answered the teacher with a smile. "But first, would you remind the class what the show-and-tell topic is for today?"

Everyone cleared a wide path as Porcupine waddled up to the front of the room. He cleared his throat and began: "We're all supposed to tell one thing God has given us to protect our bodies. What God has given me is quills! My quills are very loose, and if an enemy tries to have me for dinner . . . watch out! He'll get a mouthful of quills instead."

Suddenly the door flew open. In wafted Sally Skunk. "Sorry I'm late, Teacher," said Sally. "I had a little accident on the bus, and the bus driver passed out from the smell."

The class groaned. The teacher sighed. "Sally," she said, "God has given you a wonderful protection against your enemies, but really, you must try to be more careful around your friends."

"I know," said Sally, hanging her head. "I'm sorry."

"Well," said the teacher, giving Sally a hug, "what's done is done. Why don't you go to the washroom and wash up a bit?"

From the back of the room came the sound of muffled snoring. "It's Turtle again," giggled Hippo. "He's fallen asleep inside his shell."

"Poor Turtle," said Teacher. "It takes him so long to get to school that he's all tuckered out by the time he gets here. We'll let him sleep. We all know what his protection is anyway."

"His shell!" chorused the class. Teacher smiled.

"Toni," she said, "why don't you go next? What protection has God given you humans?"

Toni stood up and walked to the front of the room. "I'll need a chair," she said. Bear brought Toni a chair, and Toni sat down. She took off her shoes, then her socks. The class all crowded around to see.

"My protection is my toenails!" said Toni, lifting both feet proudly into the air.

"They're not very sharp," said Bear doubtfully.

"No good for digging," added Dog.

"Well, Bear," said Toni, "I don't have to rip apart rotting tree stumps looking for bugs to eat, like you do. And I don't have to dig holes to bury bones, like Dog. What I need toenails for is to play my favorite sport—soccer. It would really hurt to kick the ball if I didn't have toenails. And the ends of my toes would get all sore from rubbing against my shoes when I run. I'm glad God thought of toenails."

"Thank you, Toni," said the teacher, with a smile. "Toenails show that God cares for every part of us—from the tops of our heads right down to the tips of our toes!"

"Rows?" asked Turtle, waking with a start. "Did you say 'get in rows'?"

PRAISE TIME
The Lord will guard you from all dangers.
He will guard your life.
Psalm 121:7

PRAYER TIME
God, thank you for toenails. Thank you for the wonderful way you protect all your creatures. Amen.

U is for Unicorn

There it stood in the bright sunshine, right in the middle of the forest clearing where Una and her great-aunt Maude had come to pick blueberries. "Look, Aunt Maude!" Una whispered excitedly. "A unicorn!"

Aunt Maude chuckled. "What an imagination you have, child. There's no such thing as a unicorn."

"But it's right there, Aunt Maude! Can't you see it?"

"Of course not, child. I *do* see bushes full of plump, juicy blueberries, and I'm going to pick them!"

Una marched over to the unicorn. The unicorn nodded his magnificent head slightly, and his horn flashed light like crystal. "Well, unicorn," demanded Una, "are you real or not? Aunt Maude says no, but I can see you with my own eyes!"

"Of course I'm real," said the unicorn. "There are different kinds of real, you know. Just watch this!" The unicorn glided over to Aunt Maude, who was leaning over a bush. He lowered his horn and gave Aunt Maude a poke.

"Ouch!" said Aunt Maude, straightening quickly and rubbing the poke.

"That was the unicorn," Una said gravely.

"Nonsense, child," said Aunt Maude. "It was my rheumatism."

"What's rheumatism?" asked Una.

"It's the aches and pains I get because I'm eighty-three years old," said Aunt Maude. She went back to her picking.

"That wasn't very nice," Una scolded the unicorn. "And it didn't work. She still doesn't believe in you."

"So?" sniffed the unicorn. "Does that mean I'm not real, just because she doesn't believe in me?"

Una stared thoughtfully at the ground. Then she asked, "What about God? I heard my uncle say God isn't real."

"Silly uncle!" snorted the unicorn in disgust. "God is the most real of all. He made everything else that's real. If God weren't real, *nobody* would be real."

"You and that unicorn are having quite a chat," said Aunt Maude, coming over to Una. Aunt Maude paused for a moment, then she said, "He certainly is beautiful."

"But you said he isn't real!" exclaimed Una. "You said the poke was just your rheumatism."

Aunt Maude looked embarrassed. "I know," she said. "But I got to thinking. I don't have rheumatism!"

"So you can see the unicorn now?" asked Una.

"Plain as day, child," laughed Aunt Maude, "plain as day."

"It's about time!" said the unicorn, with a swish of his beautiful tail.

PRAISE TIME
Clap your hands, all you people.
Shout to God with joy. The Lord
Most High is wonderful. He is the great
King over all the earth!
Psalm 47:1

PRAYER TIME
God, you are the most real of all. For that
we praise you. Amen.

V is for Voices

"Please take your seats," hooted Owl. "It's time to begin."

All the creatures in the choir scurried to find seats.

Owl looked around the room. "Some creatures are missing!" he said. "Turtle? Are you here?"

"He's on his way," answered Beaver. "You know Turtle."

"How about Bear?" asked Owl.

"He's here, but he's hibernating," said Unicorn. "We'll just have to use his snore."

"Flea?" asked Owl.

"Here!" piped a tiny voice. "On Dog!"

"Thunder?" asked Owl. "Is Thunder here?"

There was a blinding flash of light followed by a deafening crash.

"Yup," said Owl, smoothing down his ruffled feathers, "Thunder's here, all right!"

"I know who's missing," exclaimed Rabbit. "It's the people who are listening to this story!"

"You're right!" said Owl. "Are they coming?"

Rabbit cupped his paws behind both ears and listened. "Some of them say they can't sing very well," he answered after a moment. "They don't think their voices are good enough for God's creature choir."

"That's what I thought about my voice," said Dog. "But God thinks my bark is beautiful!"

Rabbit listened again. "Some people say they just don't like singing," said Rabbit.

"That's what I said," grumbled Camel. "But God told me the creature choir just wouldn't sound right without a camel. He said he needed every creature's voice to sing his praise. So here I am!"

"God wants all his creatures to praise him," said Owl. "And now that everyone's here, let's begin!"

God made the crash of waterfalls,
*   and hushed the starry skies.*
He made the bubbling of the brook,
*   the worried wind's soft sighs.*
But earth had never heard a growl
*   till God thought up the bear.*
Deep seas were silent as the stars
*   till God put dolphins there.*
God made the squawks, the squeals, the
*   grunts—*
*   creation's merry song.*
The barking dog, the owl, the frog
*   delight to sing along.*
God loves each squeak, each hoot, each peep,
*   the moos, the barks, the neighs.*
But God gives earth his biggest smiles
*   when children sing his praise.*

PRAISE TIME
Let everything that breathes
praise the Lord. Praise the Lord!
Psalm 150:6

PRAYER TIME
God, thank you for our voices.
May our songs to you give you
great joy. Amen.

W is for Wings

Was Wesley Wilson ever surprised when he woke up that Friday morning! Somehow during the night he had sprouted wings. *Super cool!* thought Wesley. *Now I can fly!*

Wesley put on his baggiest sweatshirt so his mom wouldn't notice his wings. He gulped down his breakfast, called goodbye to his mom, and slipped out the door.

Once outside, Wesley pulled off his sweatshirt and unfurled his wings. He began to flap them and rose almost effortlessly into the air. *Awesome!* thought Wesley, as he climbed higher and higher. Below him he could see his whole neighborhood. The school bus was just pulling up in front of his house. "Not today!" chuckled Wesley. "Beat you to school!"

When Wesley got to school, he circled high above the playground, searching for Pudge, the school bully. Some of the kids on the playground noticed Wesley. "Wow!" they exclaimed in amazement. "It's Wesley Wilson! He's flying!"

Wesley found Pudge behind the school's dumpster, about to pound some poor little kid. Wesley swooped down on Pudge like a rocket, screaming at the top of his lungs. Pudge dropped his fists and took off like a shot. "Wow! Thanks, Wesley," said the little kid.

Wesley smiled. *Don't think I'll have trouble with Pudge anymore,* he thought.

Now Wesley was off to his real destination. In a forest about twenty miles away, a Hollywood film crew was shooting a movie about dinosaurs. On his way to the forest, Wesley passed a TV station. Someone inside the building saw Wesley through a window. A camera crew rushed out and began filming him. *Cool!* thought Wesley. *I'll be on the news!*

When Wesley reached the film site, he floated down for a closer look. Suddenly the film director looked up, and her mouth dropped open. "Come down!" she shouted. "We want to talk to you!" Wesley came down. "We want to make a movie about you," said the director. "We'll call it *Bird Boy.* We'll pay you ten million dollars. Just sign here."

Wesley reached for the pen. Suddenly a loud voice called out, "Wesley Wilson, stop daydreaming and finish your math!" It was Mrs. Bismarck, his teacher. Wesley sighed. Flying was much more fun.

Have you ever wished you had wings, so you could fly like a bird? It would be wonderful to fly, wouldn't it? But God has given us humans something far better than wings. He has given us imagination.

In our imagination, we humans can be anything and do anything we want! When we get tired of flying, we can get rid of our wings, turn ourselves into whales, and splash a while in the sea. Then we can zoom to the moon in our spaceships, or make ourselves invisible, or trek deep into the African jungle. And if we meet a roaring lion, we can travel instantly back home and be safe on the couch in the living room.

"W" is for wings, and "W" is for wonderful—imagination is a wonderful gift from a wonderful God. "W" is also for wonder: I wonder what your imagination will turn you into next?

PRAISE TIME
I praise you because you have made me in an amazing and wonderful way.
Psalm 139:14

PRAYER TIME
God, thank you for imagination that makes life so much fun. Amen.

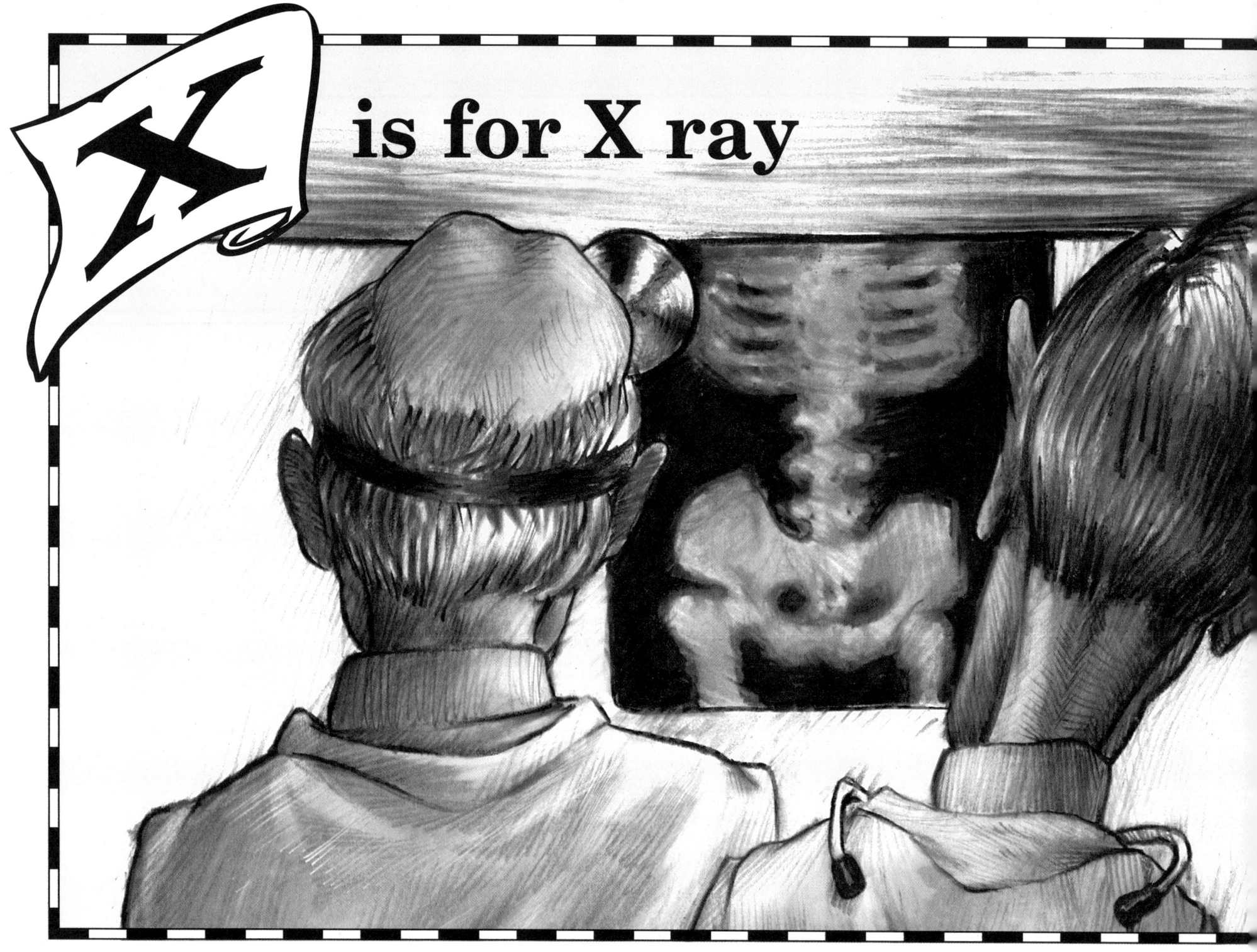

X is for X ray

Max Miller never could spell. He struggled wearily through first-grade spelling, second-grade spelling, third-grade spelling. Every night he and his mom or dad would go over the words for that week, copying, tracing, sounding out. And every time a test came, Max would fail again.

On the first day of fourth grade, Max took one look at his new spelling book and wanted to cry. Those words were impossible! He would never learn them! So Max began to cheat.

Every Thursday night, before the spelling test, Max would copy the hardest words onto a little piece of paper. Then, during the test, he would secretly copy them onto his test paper. When the test was over, Max would ask the teacher if he could get a drink. Out in the hallway by the drinking fountain, Max would scrunch the cheat paper into a little wad, pop it into his mouth, and gulp it down with water. Sure, the paper felt gross scratching its way down his throat, but Max was taking no chances.

When Max's first report card came out, his parents were delighted. "Max, you're doing great in spelling this year," they said. Max felt guilty. "Well, I guess fourth-grade spelling isn't all that hard," he lied.

Then, one Friday, Max's teacher said, "Class, next week we'll be having spelling review tests—one every day." Max thought of all the paper he would have to swallow. He groaned loudly. His teacher heard him and smiled. "You don't have to worry, Max," she said. "You've been doing so well this year!" Again Max felt guilty, but he said nothing.

The next week Max didn't go to school. All week he had a bad stomachache and diarrhea. When he didn't get better, his parents took him to the doctor. "Do you think he'll need x rays?" Max's mother asked the doctor.

"X rays?" asked Max.

"X rays let the doctor see inside you to find out why you're sick," said Max's mom.

"Oh, no!" thought Max. "If they take x rays, they'll see the paper inside me, and they'll find out I've been cheating!" Max started to cry.

"What's wrong, Max?" asked his mother. Max knew there was nothing to do but tell the truth. When he told his parents how he had been cheating, the disappointment on their faces hurt Max more than his stomach did.

"What you did was wrong, Max," said his mother. "But I don't think eating paper is why you're feeling sick."

Max's father pulled Max onto his lap. "You're feeling pretty guilty about cheating, aren't you?" he asked.

"I'm sorry," Max sobbed, hiding his face against his father's chest.

Max's mom and dad gave him a hug. "We forgive you, Max, and God will too, if you'll ask him."

Max smiled. It felt good to be forgiven. His stomach hurt a little less already.

PRAISE TIME
Happy is the person whose
sins are forgiven.
Psalm 32:1

PRAYER TIME
God, you see us inside and out, and still
you love us. We thank you. Amen.

Y is for Yes

"What would you like for breakfast?" Yolanda asked her little brother, Ramon. "Toast?"

"No!" said Ramon.

"How about cereal?" asked Yolanda.

"No!" said Ramon.

"Juice?"

"No!"

"Mama," complained Yolanda, "Ramon is impossible! All he says is 'no, no, no'!"

"Ramon's not impossible," soothed Mama. "He's just two. Two-year-olds are like that."

"You were worse, Yolanda," said Luis, Yolanda's big brother. "You were the terriblest two-year-old I ever knew."

Yolanda stuck her tongue out at Luis. "I know how to make Ramon say yes," she said. From the refrigerator she got some ice cream, and from the cupboard she got cones. She scooped ice cream into a cone and carried it over to Ramon's high chair. "Ramon," she asked with a smile, "would you like some ice cream?"

"No!" said Ramon, pushing the cone away angrily. It tumbled from Yolanda's hand and onto the floor. Yolanda reached down and put the cone on the high-chair tray.

"I was thinking," Papa said quietly. "Ramon says 'no, no, no,' but God is just the opposite. God keeps saying 'yes, yes, yes'!"

"What do you mean, Papa?" asked Yolanda.

"God is so patient. Even when we sin, he just keeps loving us and helping us. He keeps saying yes to us, like the time he sent a big fish to rescue naughty Jonah from the sea."

"I know!" said Yolanda. "God said yes to Noah and the animals when he saved them from the flood."

"God said yes to David when David fought the giant," added Mama.

"How about the time God made a path for the Israelites right through the Red Sea?" said Luis. "That was a pretty big yes."

"It was!" said Papa. "But the biggest yes of all was when God sent us Jesus."

"I think when Jesus comes back again, to get rid of Satan and be King forever—that will be an even bigger yes," said Mama. "When Jesus comes back, I think all the angels of heaven will shout 'yes! yes! yes!'"

For a moment everyone was quiet. There was a lot to think about.

Then Yolanda noticed Ramon, covered with ice cream and grinning from ear to ear. She went over to him and put her hand on his head. "Does God love Ramon?" she asked, smiling.

"Yes!" shouted Ramon.

"Yes!" agreed Yolanda, laughing and giving Ramon a big hug. "God loves Ramon, and so do I!"

PRAISE TIME

Sing to [the Lord]. Sing praises to him. Tell about all the wonderful things he has done.
Psalm 105:2

PRAYER TIME

God, you say yes to us in so many ways. Help us to say yes to you. Amen.

Z is for Zebra

Whenever Zachary Zebra's kindergarten class lined up for recess or lunch or anything else it was always the same. The Star of the Week went first, then the creatures whose last names began with "A", then the "B's," then the "C's" and so on. That was okay if you were Annabelle Ant or Bernardo Beaver, but it was not okay if you were Zachary Zebra. Zachary Zebra was always last. He was even last to be Star of the Week.

But finally his turn came. In the morning Zachary was up and had his mane brushed before his mom even came to wake him. He gulped down his bowl of shredded oats and trotted out to the bus stop.

"Good morning, Star," said Zachary's teacher as Zachary trotted into his classroom. Zachary smiled. This was his special day! He could hardly wait for recess.

When recess came, Zachary's teacher said, "Zachary, you may go first." Quickly Zachary rose from his seat and trotted toward the door.

On his way he passed Tommy Turtle. *Poor Tommy,* thought Zachary. *He's so slow that it takes him almost all recess just to get outside.* "It's okay, Teacher," said Zachary, stopping by Tommy's seat. "Tommy can go first."

When lunchtime came, Zachary's teacher said, "Zachary, you may go first." Zachary jumped up and trotted toward the front of the room. It was Pizza Day and all kinds of delicious pizza sat steaming on teacher's desk. On the way, Zachary passed Wally Walrus, who was looking very sad. Zachary remembered the last Pizza Day. They had run out of pizza after Reginald Rhinoceros, and the creatures whose names began with S through Z had gotten peanut butter sandwiches instead. "It's okay, Teacher," said Zachary. "Wally can go first."

Finally it was time to go home. "Zachary Zebra," said the teacher, "you may go first."

"Now I will go first," thought Zachary. But as he went to get his backpack from his hook, he saw Lorena Lion. That very afternoon her mother had given birth to two new cubs, and Zachary knew how eager Lorena was to see them. "It's okay, Teacher," said Zachary. "Lorena may go first."

When he got home, Zachary walked slowly into the house. "Hi, Zachary!" his mom greeted him. "How did you like being first?"

"I wasn't," said Zachary, shaking his head sadly. He told his mom what had happened.

"Zachary," she said quietly when Zachary had finished, "you *were* first today. You were first in love, and that's a lot more important than being first in line."

"Now, Zachary," said Zachary's mom, giving him a hug, "how would you like to be the very first one to try my freshly-baked oat cookies?"

Zachary smiled and took the very biggest cookie. He knew it was best to be first in love, but still, sometimes it was nice to be first in line.

PRAISE TIME
Whenever you are able,
do good to people who need help.
Proverbs 3:27

PRAYER TIME
God, we love you. Help us to be first in
loving others. Amen.